HOOD COUNTY PUBLIC LIBRARY
105197

AF580753

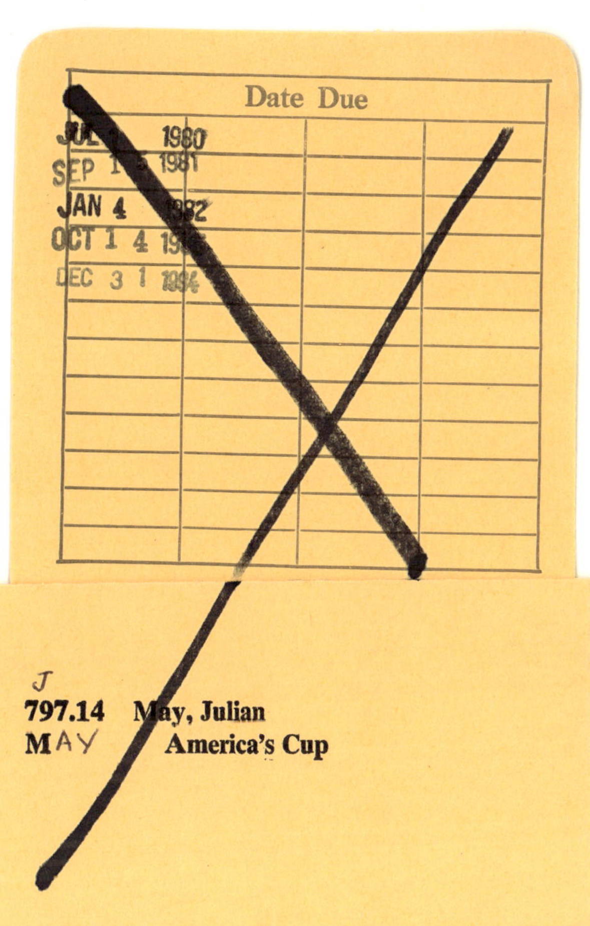
Date Due
JUL 1 1980
SEP 1 5 1981
JAN 4 1982
OCT 1 4 19
DEC 3 1 1984

SPORTS CLASSIC

AMERICA'S CUP YACHT RACE

By JULIAN MAY

Creative Education
Childrens Press

Photograph and Illustration Credits

PHOTO CREDITS:

UPI .... Cover, 1, 2, 27, 28, 29, 31, 32, 35, 37, 38, 41, 42, 45, 46
Morris Rosenfeld & Sons 8, 11, 12, 15, 17, 18, 20
Acme Photo 23

Published by Creative Educational Society, Inc., 123 South Broad Street, Mankato, Minnesota 56001. Printed in the United States.

Library of Congress Cataloging in Publication Data

May, Julian.
America's Cup yacht race.

SUMMARY: A history of America's Cup competition, the classic race between American and foreign yachts which began in 1851.

1. America's Cup races—Juvenile literature.
[1. America's Cup races. 2. Yacht racing] I. Title.
GV829.M38 797.1'4 76-8448
ISBN 0-87191-523-5

Contents

America and Her Cup

Yacht race!

Two tall-masted vessels race off Newport, Rhode Island. Sunlight sparkles on the water. A smart breeze stiffens snowy-white sails. Held back by patrolling Coast Guard craft, a horde of spectator boats crowds in to watch the action.

To millions of boating fans, this is *the* race – the classic battle between Yankee yachts and foreign challengers. It is the America's Cup competition, which began back in 1851.

Spectators peer through binoculars. Sea gulls wheel overhead as the two yachts flash toward the finish. A gun signals victory for one of the contenders. The crew breaks out the champagne, but they do not drink it from the America's Cup – which has no bottom! It is secure in the New York Yacht Club, enshrined in glory, the symbol of yachting's highest achievement.

A strange symbol it is!

The America's Cup, sole prize of the great yacht race, is an old silver trophy that looks like a skinny pitcher with a spare tire. It is not really a cup at all, but an *ewer*, a kind of old-fashioned jug that might be used for pouring wine if it just had a bottom.

Yachtsmen from many countries have spent millions of dollars trying to win America's Cup. Crews have practiced for months – even years – to be sharp for the race. Beautiful vessels have been built especially for the event; they are all but useless for any other race, or even for ordinary sailing.

The yacht America sails amid spectator craft during the great race of 1851.

The America's Cup races have been marked by keen rivalry, squabbling, bravery, hurt feelings, and excitement. Non-sailors find it hard to appreciate the event at all. American humorist Ring Lardner said, "The America's Cup races ought to be moved to the Niagara River — just above the Falls."

But lovers of tall ships feel differently! For them, the America's Cup remains the supreme challenge in yachting, the best-known sailing race in the world.

It all began back in the mid-1800's when steamships were beginning to crowd out the graceful sailing vessels that had once ruled the seas. Wealthy Britons sailed large yachts for pleasure in those days and boasted of their speed.

American yachtsmen believed the Yankee pilot schooners were capable of beating any British yacht. Some members of the New York Yacht Club decided to challenge the English yachts to a race during the great Trade Fair of 1851. They commissioned a shipbuilder named William H. Brown to construct the vessel. Brown had great confidence in his ability. He agreed that if his yacht lost, he would not be paid for building her!

The Yankee challenger was named America. She was a schooner 101 feet 9 inches in overall length with a long, sharp bow. Her masts were "raked" — that is, they slanted slightly toward the stern. Her sails were fine cotton, with a total area of 5,263 square feet.

America sailed to England and caused a furor. She was so speedy that the Royal Yacht Squadron decided it had made a great mistake in accepting the challenge. No British yacht would agree to race with

America. The London newspapers jeered at their chicken-hearted countrymen, and finally the Royal Yacht Squadron agreed to an "all comers" contest.

It was America versus anything the British cared to float! On August 22, 1851, 17 British cutters and schooners lined up for a 58-mile race around the Isle of Wight. The lonely challenger was last off the mark (she had anchor trouble), and the British spectators felt their hopes rise.

In the early part of the race, with light winds, America sailed in the middle of the fleet. But then the breeze picked up. America was able to sail much closer to the wind than the English vessels. Her taut cotton sails were superior to the baggy linen sheets used by the Squadron. She swept into the lead and stayed there until the end.

Queen Victoria watched on the royal yacht as America came speeding toward the finish. A signalman reported to her, "The American boat has been sighted, Madam."

"Indeed," said the Queen, hiding her disappointment. "And which is second?"

The sailor swept the horizon with his telescope and said sadly, "I regret to report there is no second."

America won the race by more than 8 minutes, some 2 miles ahead of the little British yacht Aurora. As her prize, she took home the "Royal Yacht Squadron 100-Guinea Cup."

Queen Victoria visited the skipper of the America at the time of the great race.

A Currier print shows the America with her raked (slanted) masts and taut cotton sails. British sails were made of flax and could only be kept taut by drenching them with water. Taut sails made America more efficient on windward legs of the race.

Some Rough Sailing

It was the fashion in those days for Britons to sneer at Americans as uncouth barbarians. When the cream of English yachts was soundly whipped by a Yankee schooner, howls of outrage echoed all over the British Isles.

"It was a fluke!" was one of the mildest things said about the race.

The American yachtsmen who had won the Cup turned it over to the New York Yacht Club in 1857. It was named a "Permanent Challenge Cup," and races for its possession could be organized by mutual consent between yacht clubs representing individual countries. No single skipper could issue a challenge; it had to be done through a club, and only a club could keep and display the Cup.

For many years, the Cup simply gathered dust. It was not until 1870 that a British yacht, Cambria, took up the challenge and sailed over for a race. The Americans had their revenge, for poor Cambria was forced to race an American fleet of 23 — including the old America.

The race took place on a 38-mile course from Staten Island to Sandy Hook lightship and back. First off was the 84-foot schooner Magic; America, once again, took off last. Cambria, a 113-foot schooner, got a good position by the time she reached the lightship; but she was clearly outclassed by the Yankees, and on the homeward leg, eight yachts passed her. Magic won, America came in fourth, and Cambria — under corrected time — finished a sorry tenth.

The owner of the Cambria, James Ashbury, was running for Parliament. He had got good publicity from the 1870 race, and he decided to come back for more the following year. This time, his boat was the 126-foot schooner Livonia. The New York Yacht Club agreed to race only one vessel at a time against Livonia — but four yachts stood ready, according to the weather conditions that might prevail. In the end, Livonia had to race the light-weather schooner Columbia and the heavy-weather schooner Sappho. The Britisher won only one of the five races.

In 1876 the Canadians had a chance at the Cup which was now variously called the "Royal Cup" or the "Queen's Cup." But the Countess of Dufferin was not to win it. Although the Canadian schooner put up a gallant try, she had not been as well-fitted as the American yacht Madeleine, which won both races. In the second race, the old America sailed the course, but not as a challenger, and beat the Countess' time by 19 minutes!

It was the last Cup race by schooners. In 1881 the Canadians challenged again, this time with a new sloop, Atalanta. The American defender was another sloop, Mischief, which won easily. However, Atalanta lost mostly because of her inept crew; she was basically a boat of American design and extremely competitive. With a better crew, she might have taken the Cup.

Atalanta had come to the race via the Erie Canal from Lake Ontario. To forestall another invasion by dangerous Canadian lake yachts, the New York Yacht Club changed the rules of the America's Cup challange. Henceforth, a challenge could be issued

Countess of Dufferin and Madeleine were similar gaff-rigged schooners. This is the start of the 1876 race. The Countess lost because of inferior sails and rigging.

only by a club having an *ocean-water* regatta, and the challenger had to arrive under sail, on her own bottom (hull). This meant that fast shallow-water yachts could be used by Americans to defend the Cup, but challengers had to compete with stronger (and slower) ocean-going yachts.

Naturally, this ruling made for hard feelings among challengers, who felt the Americans had stacked the deck in their own favor! But in 1885, the Royal Yacht Squadron sent the cutter Genesta to race. In one heat, Genesta was fouled by the American sloop Puritan. She could have been awarded the contest on a technicality, but the British skipper nobly said; "I have come for a race, not a sailover."

Genesta and Puritan put on one of the closest of America's Cup contests. England lost by using too much canvas; but both crews cheered the other, and squabbling was temporarily forgotten.

The following year featured a dull race between Scotland's Galatea and America's Mayflower. The Cup stayed safely in New York. In 1887, another Scottish yacht named Thistle tried again. She had done well in British races, but she was a flop in Yankee waters.

Once more, there was rule change. Americans stipulated that the dimensions of challenging yachts had to be published 10 months in advance. The British retorted that this information would allow Americans to "outbuild" any challenger. Finally, it was agreed that only the length of the challenger need be published. Evidently this was all American yachtbuilders needed, however, for Yankee vessels were victorious in both the 1893 and 1895 contests.

Galatea and Mayflower contended in the 1886 race. The American yacht won, 2-0.

A Fine Cup of Tea

There was a lot of bad feeling after the 1895 race. The Irish owner of the challenger, Lord Dunraven, had complained bitterly all through the series and had defaulted one race after spectators crowded his yacht. Many yachtsmen complained about the way that the race was being handled – the "unfair" rules that favored the Americans, the unruly spectator boats, the increasing cost of building yachts that could compete for the Cup.

Some people were afraid that the America's Cup races were nearly at an end. Many British yachtsmen said they would boycott the contest until the Yanks changed the rules.

One man kept the international competition from dying. He was a genial millionaire from Northern Ireland who had made a fortune selling tea. Sir Thomas Lipton was not a sailor himself, but he liked to ride on his moter yacht, and he was fascinated by the publicity potential of the America's Cup race.

So Sir Thomas built a racing yacht, Shamrock, the first of five which would bear the name, and brought it to America. The friendly tea merchant was a far different sort of Irishman from irascible Lord Dunraven. He won the hearts of American newspaper readers when he rescued a Yankee yacht in distress. Later, as the races had to be postponed again and again because of unfavorable winds, Lipton kept his good temper.

Sir Thomas Lipton's cheery face still appears on packages of tea!

Shamrock finally raced Columbia on October 16, 1899. The American vessel won by 10 minutes in fog. On the next day, both yachts raced magnificently, neck and neck, for 25 minutes. But Shamrock bore so much sail that a strong gust snapped her topmast. She could not finish and the race was lost. Repairs were made for a third race, but once again Columbia won.

Sir Thomas Lipton was undaunted, and he returned in 1901 with Shamrock II to face the same defender. This time, the races were very close. Columbia won the first heat by 1 minute 20 seconds and the second by 3 minutes 35 seconds. The third race provided a thrilling finale as the two splendid yachts pressed toward the finish almost side by side. Columbia won by 41 seconds.

In 1903, Lipton came to New York waters again with Shamrock III, a speedy cutter. In the first race, the Irish yacht was even with the American when her crew made a fatal mistake, hoisting a sail. It cost the contest. In the next two races, there was barely enough wind to move the yachts. The American, Reliance, won because she was better designed for light winds.

World War I now intervened, and it was not until 1920 that Sir Thomas raced again. Shamrock IV, the best of his yachts, won 2 races out of 5 against the American Resolute, but it wasn't good enough.

Shamrock V was the first J-class yacht to try for America's Cup.

J-Class Challenges

Despite his defeats, Lipton and his tea got excellent publicity mileage out of the Cup races. Some people even called the trophy the "Lipton Cup," since the beverage king seemed to have an exclusive franchise on its challenges!

Sir Thomas was destined to make one last try for the coveted "ould Mug." In 1930, both defender and challenger agreed to sail specially built "J-class" yachts, which meant that there would be no more time allowances. No longer would a yacht cross the finish line first, only to be declared loser when the time was adjusted.

In another important change, the site of the racing was shifted from New York to the waters off Newport, Rhode Island. The sea there was less crowded by commercial shipping and "lower class" spectator boats, and the winds were believed to be steadier.

Lipton's Shamrock V had an entirely different silhouette from Shamrock IV. Her streamlined "Marconi" rigging featured a triangular mainsail in place of the old topsail and gaff. Using less canvas, a J-boat could sail faster and with more stability than an old-style racer.

Shamrock's opponent was Enterprise, skippered by Harold J. Vanderbilt. The American J-boat closely

The 1934 American defender (top), launched in a drizzle, was appropriately named Rainbow. At bottom is the sleek hull of Endeavor II, British challenger for 1937.

resembled the yacht from the United Kingdom, but it had been prepared much more carefully. Its builder, W. Starling Burgess, tested designs in a tank and in a wind tunnel in an effort to create a perfect racing machine.

Enterprise had to lick three other speedy J-boats in order to earn the right to defend America's Cup. All through the preliminary events, Vanderbilt and Burgess added new gadgets and made fine changes until they were accused of trying to construct an "automatic yacht" that would sail with button-pushers as crewmen!

It didn't quite come to that, of course; but when Lipton's fifth Shamrock met the mechanical marvel, there was hardly a contest at all. Enterprise was by far the faster yacht and Vanderbilt the superior skipper. In the four heats that decided the challenge, Shamrock lost three races and withdrew from a fourth when a main halyard parted.

Sir Thomas Lipton, acclaimed as "the most gallant loser," withdrew from America's Cup competition after 31 years as lone challenger. He died not long after the race.

In 1934, another breed of challenger appeared. Royal Yacht Squadron member T.O.M. Sopwith had won fame as the builder of the "Camel" aircraft during World War I. He seemed just the right sort of mechanical-minded chap to lick the gadget-loving Americans at their own game!

In 1934, he challenged for the Cup with a magnificent J-boat, Endeavour. Vanderbilt, skippering Rainbow, once again had the honor of defending. Sopwith was at a disadvantage because his professional crew had gone on strike for higher wages before the yacht left for America. Two-thirds of the men had to be replaced with amateurs.

Despite this handicap, Skipper Sopwith brought Endeavour in the winner in the first two races of the series! The Americans, especially Vanderbilt, were stunned. In the third race, Endeavour built up a lead of over 6 minutes. Vanderbilt groaned, "The Cup is as good as back in England."

But fate had other plans. Endeavour ran into a "flat spot" where there was little wind. Sopwith tried to escape and only dug himself in worse. But Rainbow, with Sherman Hoyt taking over her helm, ghosted slowly up to the British yacht, passed her, and won!

Vanderbilt got a new spinnaker sail for the next race and also added ballast to Rainbow. Some sharp maneuvering by the Americans in the fourth race brought a protest from Sopwith, but victory went to Rainbow. The series was tied, 2-2.

In the fifth contest, Rainbow lost a man overboard! He clung to a line and was quickly hauled in, and the Yanks were 3 up in the best-of-7 series.

Everything rode on the sixth race. Sopwith had a minute's lead when Endeavour's rigging was fouled. The amateur crew did their best under the handicap, but lost by 55 seconds. The Cup stayed in America.

In 1937, Sopwith challenged again; but his Endeavour II was inferior in design to Vanderbilt's Ranger, which won 4-0. That was the last of the J-boat races. Not even the richest yachtsman could afford to build 135-foot sloops just to sail for the America's Cup.

Columbia Versus Sceptre

It would be 21 long years before the next challenge for the America's Cup. World War II and its recovery years put a stop to all yachting. Then there was the simple matter of finances. The lofty J-boats were dinosaurs of sail, and their day had passed. Before Cup racing could resume, lawyers had to alter the rules that governed the challenge.

Finally, the New York Supreme Court permitted two important rule changes. The first was in the size of the yachts. Henceforth, the challenge would take place between "12-meter" yachts. (The figure is arrived at after complex calculations involving many different dimensions, but the overall length of the yachts is about 68 feet, half the length of a J-boat.)

The second important change was that challengers would no longer have to sail to the race "on their own bottoms." This allowed the removal of a lot of excess weight from challengers.

The first race run under the new rules took place in 1958. The British yacht Sceptre, with a very unusual design, met the American Columbia. Columbia had earned the right to defend after a particularly exciting series of elimination races. She was designed by Olin Stephens (who would conceive four Cup winners) and crewed by men sharpened by a month's tough competition.

Sceptre had lacked the advantage of competitive practice sessions, and this was blamed for her

4-0 loss to Columbia. The British boat was roundly cheered for her sporting try, but real Cup competition would come not from England, but from the other side of the world.

Columbia (left) heads off on a different tack, well ahead of the British yacht Sceptre. A marker tug is at right during the 1958 race.

Before the actual America's Cup contest, American yachts compete for the honor of defending the trophy. In 1958 the chief rivals were Vim (right) and Columbia.

Columbia's crew gives a salute as the yacht surges toward victory.

Australians Ahoy!

Stung by Sceptre's defeat, the British planned to issue another challenge early in 1960. Before they could get their oar in, however, the New York Yacht Club received another bid for America's Cup.

It came from Australia.

At that time, the Aussies were not used to racing 12-meter yachts. But they were great sailors, willing to learn, and willing to spend the money and time that the project needed.

The yacht from Down Under was christened Gretel. She was 69 feet 5 inches long overall and had a 92-foot aluminum mast. Her sails were made in Australia from dacron imported from the United States. The Australian designer was allowed to test his models in the tank of American designer Olin Stephens.

Gretel's backers got two other 12-meter yachts for her to practice against. They were not going to make the mistake of the Sceptre people. Reports of Gretel's prowess reached the United States, and American yachtsmen began to hope that a truly exciting Cup series was on the way.

The Yankee defender was selected after stiff elimination races. The victor was Weatherly, which had tried unsuccessfully to become defender in 1958. This time Weatherly had a new keel and less topweight. In the trials, she beat not only Columbia, the old champion, but also the brand-new Nefertiti.

The largest mob of spectators ever to witness America's Cup racing turned out on September 15,

A dramatic moment during the 1962 races finds the American yacht Weatherly (right) "crossing swords" with Australian challenger Gretel.

Rival skippers in the 1962 America's Cup races are challenger Jock Sturrock of Australia (left) and Bus Mosbacher of the U.S.

1962, for Weatherly's meeting with Gretel. President John F. Kennedy, himself a yachting enthusiast, was there watching from a destroyer. Jock Sturrock skippered Gretel, and Bus Mosbacher was in charge of Weatherly.

Mosbacher showed his talent at the very beginning of the first race by out-maneuvering Sturrock over the starting line. Although the Australian pressed closely all through the heat, Weatherly came in the winner by a decisive 3 minutes 46 seconds.

In the next race, Weatherly once more grabbed an early lead. But Sturrock brought Gretel up inch by inch; and as the yachts rounded the mark, Weatherly led by a scant 14 seconds. The last leg was a run using the huge spinnaker sails. Gretel's superbly trained crew hoisted sail first and swooped into the lead.

Gretel won by 47 seconds. She was greeted by a bedlam of ship's sirens, gunfire, and spectator cheers.

Gretel had proved her superiority on a day of brisk winds. But now her skipper made a fatal mistake. He decided to wait one day for the next heat, and thus missed a lovely breezy day that might have yielded another Australian victory.

When the two rivals did meet again, sailing conditions were less favorable for Gretel. The breeze was light and fitful, and Weatherly won in a tacking contest by 8 minutes 40 seconds.

The fourth match was played in similar conditions. Gretel's valiant try resulted in one of the closest of all America's Cup finishes, but she still lost by 26 seconds.

Sturrock and his Aussies kept their spirits high for the fifth and last race, once again sailed in light winds. But after a good start, Gretel fell behind Weatherly and eventually finished 3 minutes and 40 seconds astern.

Despite Gretel's defeat, American yachtsmen praised her crew's performance above that of Weatherly. One wrote, "The Australians have given Weatherly the best fight that has been seen in an America's Cup series in years." It was agreed that the lads from Down Under might well have won if the wind had blown harder. . . .

After the first Australian challenge, the waiting British got their turn. In 1964 the yacht Sovereign, by the same designer as the ill-fated Sceptre, met the American racer Constellation. This was the first series sailed on an Olympic-style course – three legs to windward, two reaches, and one leg downwind. The series was a disaster for Britain. In one race, Sovereign lost by more than 20 minutes – the worst shellacking in a Cup race since 1886. Constellation, skippered by Bob Bavier, won 4-0.

Then it was the Australians' turn again. In 1967 they sent the yacht Dame Pattie against the American defender Intrepid. Skippers Sturrock and Mosbacher were pitted against each other once more. This time, though, rules required that sails be woven in the home country of the contestants. The Australian cloth was inferior to the American, and Intrepid won all of the races comfortably.

Intrepid stays well ahead of Dame Pattie in the 1967 contest.

12
KA 2
12
US 22

The Centennial Race

The year 1970 would mark the centennial of the first America's Cup challenge race. No less than three countries planned to contend against the United States in that historic year — Australia, Britain, and France. The English had to withdraw when they couldn't raise enough money, but the other two challengers stood firm.

The Australian group was led by Sir Frank Packer, whose Gretel had made such a gallant try in 1962. His new yacht would be Gretel II. From the time it was first built, it proved troublesome and cranky; but the Aussies were determined to whip it into shape.

The French entry, France, was financed by an eccentric billionaire named Baron Marcel Bich. He had made a fortune from Bic ballpoint pens and had entered the race because he longed for glory. The America's Cup, snatched away from the proud Yankees and taken to France, would assure the Baron of immortality!

The two challengers had to meet each other in a series of elimination races off Newport to decide which would face the American defender. Early in the summer of 1970, Baron Bich and his forces arrived. Besides the France, a pace yacht, and 35 crewmen, the Baron brought his wife and 9 children, 5 shipwrights, 4 technicians, 2 clerks, 2 divers, a butler, a masseuse, 2 pastry cooks, and a chef! He rented a large mansion and settled in in style.

The Australians did not arrive until August, when the elimination races were scheduled to take

Gretel II (left) duels with Intrepid in 1970. Gretel won the right to challenge after defeating France's entry (see front endpaper).

Intrepid shows her style during the third race of the 1970 America's Cup challenge.

place. They and their vessel were a mystery.

The American yachts had held their own elimination races earlier. The redesigned Intrepid, skippered by Bill Ficker, had won the right to defend.

On August 21, the French and Australian yachts met for the first time. The winds were fitful and scanty; but France's skipper, Louis Novarrez, brought out the best of his craft. France led Gretel II until the fifth leg of the race. There he took the turn tightly, while Australian captain Jim Hardy sailed more widely and kept his sheets filled, retaining momentum.

Gretel surged ahead, while France hit a dead spot with no wind. The Australians were victorious by 6 minutes. Baron Bich was furious at what he felt was a "mistake" by the talented Novarrez. For the second race, Bich substituted a new skipper and crew, an event which proved he knew more about making ballpoint pens than winning a yacht race.

Surprisingly, the new French crew pulled together nobly. France and Gretel II raced virtually side by side over most of the course, but the Australians managed to nose their way to victory in the end after a thrilling run for the finish.

Baron Bich was now livid with rage. Once again he fired his skipper, reinstating Novarrez. But the third race was a resounding defeat for the France. Only by winning the next four in a row could Baron Bich earn the right to challenge for the America's Cup.

"I will sail the fourth race myself!" the Baron declared. He did, too, and thus destroyed all his dreams of glory. For it was a foggy day off Newport, and the Baron and his yacht became hopelessly lost. They never even found the finish line!

Ignoring the laughter that followed his fiasco, Baron Bich helped the victorious Gretel II prepare for the actual Cup races. His two 12-meter yachts gave Gretel needed practice. During the practice sessions, it became clear that the Australian was actually the faster vessel, and deserved to be the challenger.

In the first Cup heat, with brisk winds and rain, Gretel suffered two bits of bad luck. First, a spinnaker got twisted when the crew tried to set it. Then a crewman fell overboard and had to be picked up. Intrepid won by more than 5 minutes.

After two postponements because of no wind, the second race began – with a collision! Because of the running start demanded in Cup races, both contestants must maneuver smartly at the beginning to gain a good position. This time, Intrepid was caught in a bind between the motionless committee boat and Gretel. The Aussie sloop hit Intrepid amidships and bounced off.

Later, Gretel recovered, caught Intrepid in the fifth leg, and won the race. But protests had been filed because of the earlier collision, and Gretel was disqualified. Australian fans howled that Gretel had been robbed, but the decision stood.

In the third race, with Gretel's crew still seething and not up to snuff, Intrepid came home victor by 1 minute 18 seconds. The fourth match saw the Aussies back scrapping, and they won by 63 seconds. But their rising hopes were to be doomed in the fifth race, which was a clear-cut triumph for Intrepid.

Once again, America's Cup stayed safe at home.

Spinnakers ballooning, Intrepid (left) and Gretel II round the first mark in the third race of 1970.

Gretel II lost the 1970 America's Cup contest 4-1.

Sail On, Courageous

The story goes that two yachtsmen were standing one day in front of the table that holds the America's Cup. One turned to the other and said, "What do you think we'll put in its place if some other country ever wins it?"

His friend replied; "The skull of the guy who lost it!"

There are other stories that try to analyze the reasons why people build America's Cup yachts and race them. One of Intrepid's crew said, "Everybody is mad in his own way. Putting time and money into an America's Cup challenge or defense is just another sort of madness."

Australian Alan Payne, designer of Gretel and Gretel II, noted cheerily, "I was perfect for the job. I had absolutely no experience with 12-meter yachts."

Bob Bavier, a winning skipper and publisher of *Yachting* magazine, said; "It's a fantastic sports event. More time, money, and talent go into it than into any other sailing race. And the fact that the Cup has never been lost gives it excitement – and creates responsibilities."

Despite a recession that made money hard to come by, a completely new defender was built by Olin Stephens for the 1974 Cup challenge. Courageous was made of aluminum, a brand-new hull material for 12-meter yachts. Her rival, once again hailing from Australia, was Southern Cross, also built of aluminum. Both yachts had had to overcome elimination threats from old rivals – the Aussies easily turning back Baron Bich, and Courageous narrowly winning out over Intrepid, the old champion.

So new were the two racing machines that there was no way of telling how they would measure against each other. Southern Cross was the most expensively mounted challenger in history, while Courageous was the ultimate child of Olin Stephens, genius of yacht design.

The day of the first match was foggy. It seemed that the challenger might be faster. But American skipper Ted Hood brought Courageous up to cancel a momentary Aussie lead, and after that managed to outrace the Southern Cross by a decisive 4 minutes 54 seconds.

The Australians were demoralized because they had believed their yacht to be a sure winner. In the next race, a collision was barely avoided. Once again, Cross seemed to go into the lead. But Courageous took advantage of an Australian blunder and flew ahead. The Americans won by 1:11.

Then came frustrating days of fog and windlessness. When the third race finally took place, the wind was steady; and the match a clear contest between crew skill and yacht speediness. And it was Courageous all the way, winning by a firm 5 minutes 27 seconds. The fourth race was an even more emphatic proof of American superiority. Courageous won by a margin of 7:19.

Someone said, "No one will ever take away the Cup as long as Olin Stephens is around."

But there was already talk of a new challenge, and vows of a new defense. America's Cup was still the big prize in yachting and likely to remain so for many years to come.

Tacking at the start of the fourth 1974 race, the American yacht Courageous gains a 20-second advantage over the Australian entry, Southern Cross.

America's Cup Winners

Year	Winner	Challenger	Score
1851	America (US)	Royal Yacht Squadron (UK)	
1870	Magic (US)	Cambria (UK)	
1871	Columbia (US)	Livonia (UK)	2-1
	Sappho (US)	Livonia (UK)	2-0
1876	Madeleine (US)	Countess of Dufferin (Canada)	2-0
1881	Mischief (US)	Atalanta (Canada)	2-0
1885	Puritan (US)	Genesta (UK)	2-0
1886	Mayflower (US)	Galatea (UK)	2-0
1887	Volunteer (US)	Thistle (UK)	2-0
1893	Vigilant (US)	Valkyrie (UK)	3-0
1895	Defender (US)	Valkyrie II (UK)	3-0
1899	Columbia (US)	Shamrock (UK)	3-0
1901	Columbia (US)	Shamrock II (UK)	3-0
1903	Reliance (US)	Shamrock III (UK)	3-0
1920	Resolute (US)	Shamrock IV (UK)	3-2
		J-Class Yachts	
1930	Enterprise (US)	Shamrock V (UK)	4-0
1934	Rainbow (US)	Endeavour (UK)	4-2
1937	Ranger (US)	Endeavour II (UK)	4-0
		12-Meter Yachts	
1958	Columbia (US)	Sceptre (UK)	4-0
1962	Weatherly (US)	Gretel (Australia)	4-1
1964	Constellation (US)	Sovereign (UK)	4-0
1967	Intrepid (US)	Dame Pattie (Australia)	4-0
1970	Intrepid (US)	Gretel II (Australia)	4-1
1974	Courageous (US)	Southern Cross (Australia)	4-0

SPORTS CLASSICS

WORLD SERIES
U.S. OPEN GOLF CHAMPIONSHIP
WIMBLEDON TENNIS TOURNAMENT
KENTUCKY DERBY
INDIANAPOLIS 500
OLYMPIC GAMES
SUPER BOWL
MASTERS TOURNAMENT OF GOLF
STANLEY CUP
NBA PLAY-OFFS
ROSE BOWL
AMERICA'S CUP YACHT RACE
WINTER OLYMPICS
PGA CHAMPIONSHIP TOURNAMENT
TRIPLE CROWN
AMERICAN TENNIS CHAMPIONSHIP
DAYTONA 500
GRAND PRIX
BOXING'S HEAVYWEIGHT CHAMPIONSHIP

CREATIVE EDUCATION